AFFILIATE MARKETING FOR BEGINNERS

How to Start Your Online Business as an Affiliate
Marketer

(How to Grow Your Affiliate Business From Zero
to Super Fast)

Kevin Young

Published by John Kembrey

Kevin Young

Affiliate Marketing for Beginners: How to Start Your Online Business as an Affiliate Marketer (How to Grow Your Affiliate Business From Zero to Super Fast)

ISBN 978-1-77485-193-7

Legal & Disclaimer

The information contained in this book is not designed to replace or take the place of any form of medicine or professional medical advice. The information in this book has been provided for educational and entertainment purposes only.

The information contained in this book has been compiled from sources deemed reliable, and it is accurate to the best of the Author's knowledge; however, the Author cannot guarantee its accuracy and validity and cannot be held liable for any errors or omissions. Changes are periodically made to this book. You must consult your doctor or get professional medical advice before using any of the suggested remedies, techniques, or information in this book.

Upon using the information contained in this book, you agree to hold harmless the Author from and against any damages, costs, and expenses, including any legal fees potentially resulting from the application of any of the information provided by this guide. This disclaimer applies to any damages or injury caused by the use and application, whether directly or indirectly, of any advice or information presented, whether for breach of contract, tort, negligence, personal injury, criminal intent, or under any other cause of action.

You agree to accept all risks of using the information presented inside this book. You need to consult a professional medical practitioner in order to ensure you are both able and healthy enough to participate in this program.

Table of Contents

Introduction

It would be great to earn a little money online?

Have you tried a variety of various business ideas but they failed to work.

Are you fed up with everything that B.S. Gurus are feeding you to convince you to purchase their $3000 course?

This course is designed ideal for you.

In this quick and simple course, you'll discover how you can aid others solve their problems by using an info product.

There is no need to make your own. You can join as an affiliate and promote the product by posting videos reviews.

What is the amount of capital you require? What do you go about getting $30?

If you've got that amount of dollars, then you could earn money.

You don't have any knowledge of business, seo expertise or any experience in marketing in any way.

If you are able to follow the instructions and follow the instructions, you could earn money.

Let's begin.

Chapter 1: What You Need To Know Before Venturing Into Affiliate Marketing

When I took the decision to go into Affiliate marketing I encountered many difficulties when it came to negotiating the first purchase. I've had years of work experience as a web designer, improving the design of websites, setting websites, and SEM. Being distributor was a brand new domain. The websites I worked with previously advertised the products they sold. Some had affiliate programs that they had created. While I had a few affiliate interfaces on my site but I've never thought about it enough to consider becoming an affiliate distributor.

In the event that the economy went through an economic downturn, and couple of my clients had their budgets re-established I decided to turn affiliate marketing an ongoing job. I focused on ticketing events, sports, and theater. Diversification is a type of consumption that is optional. It's also a form of idealism and, in this way it is among the last things that are given up in financial downturns.

The first time I had any offers at the beginning was the beginning of a test! My experiences and web skills eliminated the specific obstacles. In the end having people purchase tickets to games and shows all over the US was an additional learning experience!

I'm creating a second website that will focus on affiliate partnerships, promotions as well as my own inclining material. Here are some of the things I tried and the process I learned that helped me.

Work On The Timing

One common misconception corporate professionals believe about business professionals is that we work when we want to it. Business visionaries who are capable of recognizing that we'll generally be working, especially in the beginning stages. Affiliate marketing is similar. It is helpful to work or had automated procedures in place for 24 all day long until you can get your planning correct.

My ads didn't just ignore changes over time; they also did not send any traffic to the page of presentation, which is not a good thing. My website's monitoring closely revealed to me the times of the day people click through. Through some experiments I eventually was able to discern which dates and times brought the most clicks. From then on I weighed the advertisement content until I had made one sale at which point I made one transaction each week.

I was always dependent on between six and 15 sales each day. It was a huge investment to figure out the best times to sell every ticket class. People who attend shows bought tickets prior to the time. Concert-goers bought tickets in a rush as ticket sales were announced and again as the show's date approached. Season finishers bought tickets on the evening their team was progressing at the conclusion of season games. All of these lessons I learned by being attentive to my site and not only working when I wanted to.

Understand Your Audience

Put aside the time to figure out who is will purchase your affiliate deal. I once consulted with one of my customers who offered costly European trips to Americans. Their low-end excursions started with a minimum of $5,000 per night. At the time I met the group, they were running AdWords ads across the nation with no conduct nor specific focus on the demographics of the target audience to determine the budget. They didn't pay any attention to the

vital fact that their typical client received a family with a pay cheque of over $250k each year. This was in addition to an previous relaxation trips. The money they spent advertising on someone who made less was wasted. This is why there's the need to identify who is in need of your services.

Being aware of who's in dire need of your assistance is equally important as knowing who is responsible for the expense. When you have a fair knowledge of who your potential customer is, you'll be able to apply your research to alter your strategy and the content.

Tailor The Content

Prior to deciding to make the effort, my site only had a few affiliate links scattered across a few pages. The connections were not often looked at as a good idea, and the offers weren't really appropriate for the visitors to my website. My approach was in a way like an angling venture to capture stray shots instead of an engaged audience.

When I developed web-based material that was line with the type of tickets I wanted to offer, my business grew up. I purchased additional space names to modify the content to suit the show or entertainer. I worked for hours creating page content and connections to my target audience. At a certain point, I had 200 websites. Two websites had all the concepts on them. The other websites were extremely custom-fitted which offered tickets to one particular event or group. Ten of them were responsible for more than 80% of the sales.

Video recordings are probably the most effective method to tell the story or demonstrate the product. The addition of videos to your welcome pages can make those who visit your site more comfortable and allows them to build trust with prospective customers. Videos recorded by cell phones are extremely acceptable provided that the images are clear and clear. The quality of the sound is fantastic If they are stableness whatsoever.

Make use of recordings to demonstrate the way your product is effective, which can be very helpful. They also add excitement to your site and help users navigate the page.

Set Up Tracking

There's no way to have excessive information! The more you consider your application visitors and your websites the more effectively you can customize your content. Include research and online life-related information on your site. It is easy to determine the country that people who visit your site come from, which promotion is successful, and what internet life channels are the most effective! In addition, you can save time and money.

Make sure you update your security strategy to show all the subsequent steps.

Make It Easy

It is applicable to all forms of marketing. The more simple to make it for site or guest on an application to buy and pay for, the more money you can earn. If your website is difficult to navigate and the guest has to purchase it from simple stacking pages as well as boring log-in pages take an effort to allow users to navigate your site prior to moving on to marketing.

A number taken from one of my counseling clients that showed us each step to enter credit card information caused clients to drop off at the rate of 25 percent per click! Ouch. Let your customers go through the hassle of using your site through an annoying shopping carts or registration, and watch your business suffer. Install the following steps and find out where the site's issues lie.

Go To Your Audience

Because you know the place your visitors come from, connect them with the place they are online. Your usual resolution should be not to rely on Facebook as a primary social media application. It is likely that they are using Instagram as well as various other platforms for social media.

If you're struggling to find time or aren't able to deal with a multitude of channels (naturally or with a premium) you should focus on a few channels the channels, master them, and then begin another. Begin with the channel you're most comfortable with and be sure to confirm before moving to the next.

Be wary of stagnation and being limited to a single social media site. If your usage arrangement is changed or is more troubling your account is hampered and you may be in a position where you are not able to use the mediums of your choice. Make sure you have an account on at least 2 social networks, like, for example, Facebook and AdWords, to increase the chances of connecting to a bigger market and offering plenty of choices.

Try not to Be To Sales

I have a close friend that is "that person." The person is Amazon affiliate. His Instagram account is 100% product shots. His Facebook page hasn't significantly enhanced. I removed him from my feed in the past year because I was annoyed by his charismatic abilities and his actions didn't seem to seem to me to be authentic. There wasn't one single photo of him using one of these tools or even a hospitable websites, or an online survey. His online life was a relic of the past and I'm guessing that his business wasn't performing well.

Do not try to bribe your customer with money each time. Always offer them other useful services. When it came to ticketing for special occasions this was extremely easy. I would send them messages advising them about the past purchases, published the scores of games for sports enthusiasts and tweeted out the consequences of spoilers in entertainment to theatregoers. I was always on their minds when they needed to purchase a ticket. If I had been trying to convince them of something at every opportunity, I could be on their list of blockers.

Keep Up With Technology

Innovation evolves, so must you. Are you aware of the 200 websites I mentioned? Seven years ago they were earning money. Today they are what's now known by the term "Slim content" websites. That means Google.com is not thrilled with my SEO Ninja tricks and has moved my websites down a few pages of the SERPS. So, I have refocused my method and have since seen more actively engaged websites that have significantly increasing information.

If you're using the web-based version of SEM or life, in the habit of keeping your website up-to-date, especially when you are offering anything that falls under adult-oriented categories such as gambling or liquor. The amicable and flexible configuration has evolved to become "portable first." The security of websites through SSL is now one of the many SEO ranking elements. Google alters its algorithm frequently So, make sure you purchase a few brochures and establish an affiliation with your account administrator. They can also inform you about refreshes.

Authenticity Matters. Sell What You Are Passionate About.

Our opinions are influenced by verbal advice. buying decisions. We're bound to buy (or not) because of the thoughts of other people In any case, in the event that an audit comes from an outsider who is completely uninvolved. This is why influencer marketing is so effective!

The authenticity of your affiliate program is proven when you include products and details that you like and use. It will also help you avoid tiny substance sites! Selling something you believe in can work magically.

Seek Out People That Support Your Vision

I was having lunch with a good friend of mine, and I revealed the fact that I am currently an affiliate marketer full-time. While he didn't make any comments, I could see the disapproval rapidly wash over his face. He was a dependable physical businessman who did not feel that the need to have a conversation about business with someone who he thought to be unworthy I'm yours truly.

While I know I could have benefited in a number of ways from him but I was able to overcome it and looked for others who were more competent and knowledgeable than I was and I learned as much as they could about me. Finally I had become a successful distributor! I had websites that were top-selling and was able to let them run themselves while enjoying a vacation at the Caribbean. Do not look for people who won't be supportive of your vision.

Chapter 2: Finding A Profitable Affiliate Program

Once you've chosen the business niche you wish to serve this is the ideal time to select the profitable equipment of this process.

There are two options:

Or you can select an affiliate program, or

If you are a member of an affiliate network. Let's go over the affiliate networks in a separate way.

An affiliate program is which allows the trader to utilize an affiliate framework to create with its affiliates. Affiliates will collaborate together with the seller DIRECTLY. There will not be an external party, and no representatives to speak with. The seller is the one who will give affiliate links out, hand out products to aid in the promotion of the products and then pay the affiliates for their bonus.

An affiliate network, it's an organization that affiliates is able to join. After deciding, an affiliate will have access to hundreds, perhaps thousands of items from a variety of merchants. The affiliate can select which product to promote. Affiliate networks act as a mediator between affiliates and vendors. There are advantages and disadvantages to every choice. Affiliate networks are the ideal choice for people who aren't able to choose which product to market. With the wide range of choices offered by affiliate networks and the ability to choose any product at any time they choose, affiliate networks can provide possibilities for prospective affiliate marketers.

What's the issue?

Millions, if perhaps thousands of people are part of the exact same affiliate networks they have thought of. This means thousands, or even millions of potential customers for every product you select from a particular affiliate network. The secret to success online is actually quite simple. It could be reduced by the mathematical formula under the appeal of a product plus very little competition = the highest profits

This applies to any company. Affiliate networks might provide a popular product however, should many affiliates are advertising the product, your chances of success are significantly diminished. However, this doesn't mean it doesn't mean that you cannot succeed if you're within an affiliate program. By absorbing the lessons that follow you'll be able to raise your humour and gain a foothold on the subject of affiliate marketing despite the fact that you'll be competing with numerous affiliates.

Today, let's move on the subject of affiliate program. Affiliate programs, obviously offers fewer items for you to promote. You'll be limited to sole products offered by the merchant. In reality affiliate programs use fewer affiliates. This means less competition. Additionally, it implies more opportunities to be successful. Not satisfied by the sales rates of one particular product sold under the banner of an affiliate program? It's not a problem!

You can join a variety of affiliate programs! There's no limit with the amount of affiliates you are able to join. Additionally, almost every member program is allowed to join. They don't charge any fee for your membership. Once it's all done and dusted you're the person who helps the seller sell his goods. You are the one who has to be paid! There are a lot of fantastic affiliate programs. However, there are bad member programs. What are the best affiliate programs to steer clear of?

Be on the lookout for indications:

The product is low-quality. It may be a solution to the need in one place but due to its poor quality discounts will be pushed into. You might be able to sway a few sales but the discounts will negate the bonus. Even more troubling, you could lose credibility with your customers in directing them to a shoddy product.

The product is difficult to provide. This is self-informing. You'll not be able to comprehend your payment when the product you're required to offer is one that is a "hard offer."

The membership program has been known to not make payments to its associates. It is the most frustrating thing to be working for something only to be disqualified from winning the prize due to reasons that are not known or for a different reason.

Affiliate programs have a questionable track record in managing its clients and associates.

Affiliate networks are in a battle with regards to its finances.

Affiliate networks are continuously managed by a single or people who are not willing to display themselves.

If you spot an affiliate program that has one of these characteristics, you should run in the opposite direction. Now, how do you choose the best affiliate program? The ideal affiliate program must include the majority, if not all of the following qualities:

A hot-offering product. In the end, this is my main concern. I'm not able to succeed as a participant if I'm not able to sell any product in the first place, right? So, I typically look for programs that offer products with a proven worthiness in a particular business or, in any case the products provide a lot of guarantees.

Free commission plan. This is an option that is not required to the variable mentioned above. The commission rate that I base on I am using is 12. Anything less could require greater attention. This shouldn't be a problem but, since most membership programs pay a half commission on every sale these days.

A program well recognized for its credibility. Who needs to associate their lives with the glimmer skillet and transient stations would you not think? Do you need to be a pro? Be a loyal follower of a winner! You'll need to rely on the advice of others and your own particular effort of perseverance to locate as an affiliate programme.

A program with an excellent post-sales program. Affiliate advertising is where discounts are your enemies. It is possible to convince yourself that you've stowed an item, but should discounts are requested in the future, you will not receive any compensation.

A program with a high post-sales support can limit the demands of post sales and consequently, be able to guarantee your diversions.

In the way affiliate networks are concerned, www.cj.com, www.linkshare.com and www.clickbank.com are great places to start with. They can provide you with an array of amazing products that you can choose from, and they offer high commissions, too.

Chapter 3: The Best Affiliate Programs

Affiliate programs work using a variety of pay models, and two are that are most popular: Cost Per Sale (CPS) and the Cost Per Action (CPA).

CPS is able to pay certain amount to the marketer, who may introduce a lead which will eventually lead to the purchase. The purchase itself that generates the commission so CPS is essentially free marketing. The payout commission is usually extremely appealing.

CPA depends on a specific step performed by the person who is who is referred to as the Advertiser. It could include impressions, registrations, sign-ups, clicks, opt-ins and submission of forms. Be aware that this kind of model isn't a high-paying one. This is due to the fact that direct sales aren't an essential requirement for commission.

There are numerous affiliate programs on the Internet that one can be confused on which one to select on the site. These are affiliate programs that have earned been praised for their ease of use, and also have appealing commissions.

The ClickBank. It is enormous and boasts a library of over 6 million items that are available to many millions of users around the world. The main focus of the company happens for digital data products.

Amazon Associates. Amazon has earned a reputable reputation as the biggest online retailer in the United States. There are over one million items that can be marketed to consumers as well Amazon Associates will offer up to 10% of advertising charges.

RevenueWire. This affiliate network is a global network with a presence in greater than 100 different countries. It offers digital goods and is a genuine worldwide e-commerce platform.

Flexoffers. The thing that makes the affiliate program distinct is their commitment to providing customer service. Marketers can anticipate to be provided with tools for data delivery, as well as payments that are on time. The aim is to establish a an arrangement that's profitable for both of the parties.

eBay. It is another Internet retail giant that boasts an excellent affiliate network. What makes the eBay the partner network so attractive is the reporting, tracking, and top-of-the-line tools marketers can make use of.

There are many others, however what you need to know now is that a particular affiliate program might not be the one you require. ClickBank doesn't mean much if you are not selling digital information products. While the concept of having an international e-commerce platform is appealing however, if you focus exclusively on your United States consumer market it isn't as important to you. Studying different affiliate networks involves focusing on the your customer service and the way you will receive your commissions (PayPal for instance, is a very simple method to receive your commissions, and funds can be easily transferred from this site to the bank account you have.).

If you're blogger There are a variety of affiliate programs apart from the ones mentioned above that could be appealing to you. They include:

Google AdSense. This is part the Google family of products and has minimal requirements to be a user to take part. Google AdSense permits posting to other languages and you can anticipate ads to appearing in your web page within a matter of minutes after receiving the code for your ad. Google AdSense does have a high share of revenue for advertisers.

CJ Affiliate (Commission Junction). It has been described as a one-stop shop since there are so many big merchants who have a presence on this. There is a net 20 payment plan that guarantees the payment of commissions each month.

Neverblue. Signing up for this affiliate network is extremely easy and provides a personal tracking system. It offers a huge range of deals you can choose.

PeerFly. The affiliate network provides a range of methods of earning commission and offers a variety of payment options to select.

ShareASale. It's home to over 4000 merchants. You are likely to receive the payment by the 20th day of each month. It's also simple to evaluate different offers within this program.

LinkShare. It is a system that automatically rotates of banner ads for a given product. This makes management more simple for you. However, one issue is that it is a very small network. It is important to be aware that you will receive your money after the seller has received commission.

Chapter 4: What To Do Before Diving In

"Give me six hours to chop down a tree and I will spend the first four sharpening the ax."

- Abraham Lincoln

The above quote, which was attributed by Abraham Lincoln, is one of the most useful tips anyone could take before embarking on a undertaking. It is reasonable to think that six hours of cutting down a tree using an axe, particularly for those with little or no experience, is way too small. A person would instantly be enticed to start slashing at the wood with or her strength until the very last minute. This is, in reality, going to be the most difficult and inefficient method to do it. In addition, even the strongest lumberjacks who have an ax that is dull would struggle to cut down a tree in such the span of a few minutes. The quote is arguably a reminder of the importance of putting in lots of time and effort to studying something prior to taking a plunge.

While Affiliate Marketing isn't an exact science, you'll have to know a lot about it prior to attempting to get involved. Like every other business that you are in, you must be aware of how the company operates as well as the rules for the various players, where you can find the most effective products, and the best ways to market. Businesses such as Affiliate Marketing have not been around for a lengthy time, which is why it is essential to be aware of all that you know about the subject in order to have a shot at gaining the maximum benefits.

In the beginning one, anyone wanting to go into affiliate marketing must to know what niche that he or she is interested in most and the best place to look for it. Additionally, they must be aware of what competitors are doing and what they are doing to offer customers a better price and make use of current technology to help make the process easier.

How to Search for the Best and Most Profitable Niche

Affiliate marketing is among the most legitimate methods to earn money online. If an individual is able to master the fundamentals of the marketing procedure, it provides the greatest flexibility as well as the highest chance of earning. But it's not a fast-track to riches. Marketing through affiliates is a type of business similar to any other. This means that it requires the time, effort and perseverance to expand. Recognizing that it might take a bit of time to reel big profits is crucial to manage expectations early However, it's important to know the most effective methods of reaching one's full potential.

A niche is defined as the interests, services or products which appeal to a specific and specific segment of the population. The success of affiliate marketing can be contingent on the selection of the right and most lucrative niche. The selection of a area of study can make a massive impact on the success of affiliate marketing, therefore, it is essential to make the effort to search for the best niches and then begin using them. The main reason it's important is that certain types of products and services are sold better than others that means they have greater potential for profit.

As important, the selection of an area of interest will aid affiliate marketers in creating their own brand identity. People who attempt to sell everything from golf clubs to toothpaste do not have a distinct brand name. It is best to either be the toothpaste person or the golfing person, which can make it easier to build an image, a brand, and an audience.

The scope of a website can be wide However, subsets are generally more effective. For instance, a site that is about sports is not appropriate. So, perhaps one should concentrate on basketball, soccer or another sports. However, this could still be too broad, so one could go deeper and narrow the focus to European soccer. Finding the right niche could be a lengthy and challenging process.

How to Identify a Good Niche

If you are looking for the most lucrative areas for affiliate marketing potential affiliate marketers must look further and determine:

What are they most passionate about There is a good chance to succeed in a particular field that you are actually keen on rather than one that doesn't excite you.

What are affiliate programs offering? It is crucial to understand what affiliate programs are offering , as in some cases they might not cover the specific niche that you are interested in.

What is the subject matter that people are knowledgeable about? The list of niches that your favorite affiliate programs offer It is ideal to focus more on the one you are the most familiar with rather than niches that you aren't sure about.

What's in high-demand The market research you conduct will help you identify the niches that have the highest demand. Selecting these areas will allow to have a chance of generating healthy sales for your company.

Niches that aren't flooded with affiliate marketers . Despite the fact that those niches with highest demand also have the most affiliate marketers, it's possible to find a niche which has a lot of demand but doesn't have too many affiliate marketers competing for the same slice of cake.

There are many services that can assist people in finding good affiliate marketing programs in their particular niche. However regardless of whether one chooses not to utilize these services, the amount of affiliate programs that one can pick from range from the hundreds of thousands. There is plenty of choice.

Finding the perfect niche to affiliate marketing

When it comes to deciding the right field for an individual's needs they must consider the following:

See What is Popular

Check out the online listings of the most popular websites, like Amazon in order to gain an knowledge of what's hot. Social media websites can provide an insight into is popular and discussing. Knowing what's popular can aid in identifying the most lucrative and most lucrative areas to pursue.

Meet like-minded people

It is essential to know your circles. For instance crafting, in general, are not a big market. But, those who are fascinated by it are eager to meet people who share the same interest and look at the best and most innovative products that are available in their field. Making one's name known within these circles will aid in identifying the products or services that have been gaining greater interest.

Take a Training Program

A wealth of information is accessible online to help users understand affiliate marketing. For those who are new to affiliate marketing, they may be unsure of how to start. It is recommended to enroll in an educational program to master the art of choosing a specific niche, search for the most effective affiliate programs, design an online presence, conduct market research, write amazing content, and truly achieve success on the internet.

Use Google

Once you have selected a niche It is crucial to enter it into Google together with the affiliate course or training program. This will provide a wide range of choices to select from. If not work, you may have to pick a different niche.

Look Deeper and Analyze the Sales Pages

Before deciding on a particular subject, it is necessary to go through the web pages of sales for the products or services offered to find out if the buyer really is aware of what the niche is all about.

It is crucial to recognize that trends change and disappear. Even if a subject is popular today does not mean that it is going to be tomorrow. Therefore one must be aware of the best time to switch to another. At some point, one might need to pick a new niche when the one they are currently in does not gain ground. Certain niches that will never go out of fashion include:

Money and Wealth

Fitness and Health

Romance

It can take a while to discover the ideal and most lucrative niche. In reality, many run into a variety of obstacles before they come to a good niche. Thus, regardless of how the length of time you have to wait, don't give up hope. Also, selecting an appropriate niche is equally important as having excellent content. It is important to choose an effective combination of a profitable area and good content.

Learn from Your Competitors

Entrepreneurs who succeed have a variety of options for living life to the maximum. Due to the decrease in dependence on brick and mortar companies and the growing industrialization as well as the growth of the online business market and affiliate marketing specifically, is set to grow beyond what any could imagine. Nowadays, online entrepreneurs compete with multi-billion dollar businesses and other entrepreneurs. To stand out and survive in this crowded and competitive market, they must utilize effective and efficient marketing tools.

For many people, competition are seen as a threat to conquer. But the truth is that healthy competition isn't good. In fact, it's through it that improvements and new ideas are created. But, these are only possible in the event that one can manage and react to competition with the correct manner. This is particularly true for competition in the realm in online businesses. Through gaining knowledge about your competitors and attempting to come up with the most effective and efficient strategies, you can profit from the competition. Affiliate marketers are usually amazed by how much they could learn from competitors.

Competition in Affiliate Marketing

Affiliate marketers can make use of a variety of tools to excel in the realm in the world of revenue-based commissions. These marketing tools help marketers to comprehend the market, make money from those who visit their websites and draw more visitors. The reasons you should think about starting an online businesses like affiliate marketing are as follows:

Flexibility in work

Low capital investment

Global market

No shipments , warehousing or shipping

Ability to earn passive income

The ability to work on everything by yourself

For example they can promote a broad variety of services and/or products through their websites. They have the option of choosing from membership possibilities, different services, physical items and digital goods from all over the globe. Over the past 10 years or thus networks have been one of the major factors behind the development of the market.

Today, individual marketers as well as networks are experiencing changes that could weaken their influence over the marketplace. Certain large corporations are shifting the administration of affiliates into their own departments and eliminating affiliate networks. Additionally, companies that specialize in search marketing and media are steadily entering the industry by through their existing relationships with customers. With the number of companies and individuals that are involved in affiliate marketing, it's easy to understand why novices and experienced affiliate marketers are anxious.

It is a fact that any person can achieve success in this industry regardless of the degree of competition. Affiliate marketing isn't so much about battling it out against others who are affiliate marketing. It is, in fact, more about the way one markets affiliate products and/or services to their target audience. The fundamentally, one's marketing abilities are more important than their ability to compete. However, competition is beneficial for any business.

The lessons we can learn from our competitors in the business world online

Analyzing competition can help improve their marketing strategies and methods of conducting business to differentiate oneself from the rest of the pack. The knowledge gained will allow one to develop creative marketing strategies which take advantage of the limitations of competition while enhancing one's performance as well. This will help become more real. To understand what competitors are doing it is necessary to take a look at:

How do you leverage technology?

They offer the products or services they offer

How do they market their products to their customers

They employ tools to improve customer satisfaction

Their business strategies

Their media-related activities

It is also advisable to learn the most information you can about the customers of your competition such as:

The items and/or services they purchase

Who are they?

If they have customers who are faithful

What they observe in each of their competitors

An in-depth analysis of this information can help one decide what they can do to make the most of the market more effectively. It can also reveal if there is a lot of competition in particular segments of the market which could help to shift on to niches with less competition. This is particularly relevant in the case of affiliate marketing.

This information is likely to fall into one of the categories below:

What can competitors do better than competitors?

What are they doing at the same thing

They are not far in comparison to

When competitors are doing better, one has to adapt to the competition and devise efficient changes, like altering the marketing strategy and updating the products as well as services, and even redesigning the website. The key to success is in the process of innovation and not imitation. If their performance is identical to one's then one must find the reason for this.

It is essential to research any commonalities to determine if there is room to improve. This is due to the fact that they could be planning to do something similar. However If they're failing in one way or another it is important to do all possible to make use of those weaknesses.

In today's business environment the competition has an important role. It's not just to make it harder for companies to achieve success. It usually helps people improve their performance to be successful.

Word tracker (Keyword Tool)

When it comes to improving the SEO of a website and increasing its credibility as a brand and blog One will encounter a variety of ways to get the message across. Word tracker is among the most trusted tools for media outreach on the market. This tool can help in reducing time and effort during study by providing over 2,000 of the most often used or searched for keywords on the internet within a single search.

Word tracker is among the top tools to research keywords you can utilize to discover profitable niches and find out what keywords your business's competitors are using. Additionally, it is able to produce ten thousand keyword phrases per query, and include the related keywords. This provides online marketers with the capability to enhance their website pages better to rank higher than their competitors. This tool is beneficial and can be used in a broad spectrum of online business operations that include identifying the most lucrative and most lucrative niche that affiliate marketing is a good fit for.

How it Works

This tool can help entrepreneurs on the internet to increase their earnings and expand their business through the following methods:

Time to save

Creating reliable keyword results

Exploring new, potentially lucrative market segments that could be profitable

Optimizing SEO rankings

Attracting lucrative, targeted web traffic

When it comes to increasing SEO ranking, for example, Word tracker generates results that are based on real searches made by real people, such as people who want to purchase something. Additionally, it utilizes an authentic database that has access to the most recent information on search results. This is especially important in the search for reliable marketing data. For instance, to improve the visibility of their website or blog affiliate marketers should not be able to guess what their audience is attracted to. They simply have to base their choices in deciding the right niche, based on information.

This tool goes into depth to find the keywords that people actually use in their Internet search results. Users are able to limit their searches to the state or geographical zone within both the US and UK which gives them more precision.

With its huge data base, Word tracker gives users the chance to connect with more people and takes the burden out of research. In today's highly competitive online business world, accuracy and efficiency can be an enormous difference in the outcome or failure. Through improving the effectiveness of keyword search, making it more efficient quicker, simpler, and easier the tool will improve your website's performance and visibility without having to sacrifice much work and energy.

Additionally, it helps entrepreneurs online understand what customers are searching for on the internet Keyword research can aid them in determining the potential and the size of the demand or market for any product or service. Many successful online entrepreneurs realize that the online marketplace is full of unexplored opportunities in the niche. This is why they utilize tools for keyword research such as Word tracker to find and capitalize on these opportunities that are not being explored.

Most successful marketers understand the truth is that competition isn't always good. It is more important to know what they take away from their competitors. For affiliate marketers, as an instance could make use of Word tracker to get an accurate view of competition for the specific phrase or word that will allow them to determine the degree of competition in a specific market segment. Thus, they'll be able know the difficulty it is to be ranked high in Google search results, and ideally at the top of page.

How do I make use of Word tracker

Register for an account with no cost

Log in using your username and password.

Input your seed keyword choose your region and then click search.

Sort the results according to the level of competition

Explore deeper to uncover any long-tail key words

Utilize the wildcards to increase the amount of keywords.

Remove any irrelevant keywords

Keep the relevant keywords

Create a new video or article for each keyword.

If one makes use of this tool to dig into a keyword's lengthy tail and find the longest tail, it is possible to find the most popular phrases or sentences that incorporate the keyword used to create the seed. For example, a Google search for the term contemporary can result in results like Contemporary furniture and music and many more. Related keywords however don't always include the primary keyword. For instance, eyeglasses will result in keywords such as sunglasses, bifocals, frames and even different brand names of manufacturers of eyewear.

When you are trying to navigate the confusing and sometimes complex field of marketing online, it is essential to be able to count on solid support and knowledgeable resources at any time one requires them. Word tracker provides great service and support 24 hours a day and includes:

Free online tutorials

Live chat or phone support with a knowledgeable helpdesk

Many how-to articles within their academy for free.

A weekly webinar designed to introduce people to its capabilities

There are a variety of free tools to research keywords online However, many are only suitable for faulty and unpaid searches. They don't provide the depth of information that marketers require to boost their income and perform better in comparison to their competition and drive more traffic. The online world isn't getting any simpler or less overcrowded. Failure to implement efficient SEO methods could result in a loss of a sale and a customer lost each day.

Chapter 5: Create A Product Review

There isn't a "set in a stone" formula to write video reviews , however I've discovered some techniques and crucial aspects that you must be discussing in order to write an excellent review of a product.

Here are my seven guidelines to write a review of a product.

Be aware that you don't need to follow or implement all of them within one video.

But the more you choose to use in your video the more effective your video will be.

#1 - Educate and then sell

Many people will immediately test and market the product. They tell them about the advantages of the product, and then make them buy it.

This isn't going to be a success.

There's too much competition , and you must be more competitive than your competition!

The most effective solution is to inform your audience initially about your product.

Let them know:

What is the name of the product?

What is it that they do?

How how long have you used it for?

Does it work? What is the reason?

Have you recommended it your friend?

#2 - Use HD if Possible

We can't all pay for HD cameras , which are extremely expensive.

The best camera you could utilize is the one you already own.

Make use of your iPhone or any other phone you own.

Today, most phones have decent video quality so long as you get the correct angle and the proper lighting.

#3 - Say the Pros and Cons

Do not just talk about the pros but don't make it seem like a believable. Include some cons, but clearly don't talk about important factors that could be considered to be a deal breaker.

In any case, I'd guess that you'd only suggest anything that works and is actually beneficial.

4. This might be the right choice for you If... You're not sure this isn't the right choice suitable for you If...

One of the most effective strategies I've discovered from reading hundreds, if more than thousands of product reviews is that if you inform the reviewers if they should purchase it or not the product will be loved by them and purchase the item through that link (amazon associate URL).

Include a segment of the video devoted to explaining to them whether they should purchase the product or not.

#5 - Recommend a Substitute

If the product isn't an ideal fit for them you can suggest a replacement product that is the best fit for the user.

In this way you'll have the chance to market a different product. (You'll include the Amazon affiliate link in the video)

#6 - Tell a Story

When you've got an engaging tale or have an acquaintance who has had the product previously. Share with them your experiences having the program.

People are looking for someone they can connect to.

Don't become a robot ....

These are the benefits...

These are the negatives... Bla bla

Tell them a story that is related to your product, and they'll be thrilled!

#7 - Call to Action

Request that they purchase the product through your link!

Don't be afraid to do this. Honesty is the best policy.

Inform them that you'll earn an affiliate commission if they purchase through that link.

If your review is truly valuable, they'll share your review and will be delighted to do the same for you.

EXAMPLES:

What is Batiste Dry Shampoo?! Report and Demonstration

Here are some videos on Youtube which you could use as models to promote your own business.

https://www.youtube.com/watch?v=-_EDzRNCHq8

https://www.youtube.com/watch?v=QSOXVz9up5k

https://www.youtube.com/watch?v=2pFAr6hgIEM

https://www.youtube.com/watch?v=ZNHTX1qIuPs

Chapter 6: How To Earn Your Rst Dollar Today In Af Liate Marke Ng?

Choose Your Products

The first choice you could make about affiliate marketing on the internet is what products to advertise. Each comes with their own pros and cons of selling them on the internet. For many it's an individual choice or a factor that is contingent on the field of study they wish to venture into.

In the beginning it might be easy to go through a particular section that you're for even if it might not be an effective one.

Do your best to do your research and you'll be able to quickly identify areas of interest that aren't too demanding, but can earn you good affiliate income as you set up your website and start getting people to it.

Provide A Solution To A Problem

It's important to remember that typically, affiliates shouldn't be advertising something. Many entrepreneurs fall for this mistake when they're just beginning their journey on the internet.

While you may think you're selling something, the truth is that you could be just prominent customers of the web page for the product that you may be selling.

DIY Teeth Whitening ♡ My Favorite!

The person who owns the products or services is likely to have spent a of thousands of dollars on their sales and marketing copy, therefore you should always leave the promotion to them.

The only thing you can do is present your site's visitors with the appropriate solution to the problem.

Are People Ready To Buy?

If you've discovered an area that has many monthly searches it is essential to know whether the users are required to buy something.

If they're simply seeking information It's unlikely that you'll earn any cash.

The best niches can include a variety of products that you could promote them via affiliates. You can check this out through ClickBank.

Prospector's Gold Rush Hair Pomade Review

If your subject of interest is related to data-related products it is essential to find at least a few inventories on the web. If you're in an extra segment for physical goods, you can try Amazon.

How to Generate Traf c for Your Affiliate Markeng Website?

Traffic is one of the most important aspects of your affiliate marketing company.

Whatever you think your website's performance could be or how well products you offer however, you're not making money if you don't have any customers. There are totally different strategies you could employ to bring visitors to your site.

Earn Your
First
Dollar $

Many have a question after they have started selling their site is:

Do I have to use paid or free visitor's strategies?

Free Traffic

Free strategies for visitors are the method that most affiliate entrepreneurs choose to begin. They do this due to the fact that they are unable to access the funds to invest in their business.

It's extremely likely to make significant money using free strategies for visitors. The search engine optimization is a dependable method to rank your site high in results of searches for the most popular keywords in your region of importance.

For example, if your website is focused on canine-related coaching books, you could make your content content as well as meta specifics and other off-page and on-page search engine marketing around the term " dog training books."

This way, Google and different engines like Google could have no doubts about the subject matter of your site.

If you have good one-way links and related, top quality content material, you will be able to get your website on the top of the results of a search which is will be seen by the majority of people who searches for your specific search term.

Generate Traffic To Site

Forum advertising is an additional efficient and cost-effective method to attract visitors. This involves becoming an active member of boards that are that are related to the field that is relevant to your site. If you're a part of and become enthusiastic by sharing top-quality information it is possible to gain diverse members' opinions.

Inscribing a link to your website within your message on the discussion forum allows it to be viewed by the public each time you create a brand new installation.

I would advise you to focus on SEO and gain FREE traffic organically rather than trying paid traffic.

Get access for free to SEMrush to keep your website on the first page on Google Ranking.

Paid Traffic

Pay-per-click strategies for customers are usually the first thing affiliate marketers invest money in when they have money to put back into the business. You must learn everything you can on paid advertising.

Because of this, it being possible to lose quite many dollars in a short amount of time If you're not prudent. But, strategies for paid visitors can be more lucrative, and faster in earning your money, than other methods that are free. Pay Per Click advertising also known as PPC could be the most popular method of paying visitors for affiliate business owners. Google AdWords is an instance of PPC.

This involves placing bids for the keywords that are relevant to your goal and putting up your website. If someone searches for a term that you are focusing on your advertisement will appear in the search results. The location of your advertisement will depend on how much you're bidding against the bids of other entrepreneurs.

If you're looking for an immediate results, you could opt for Simpletraffic.com for their paid traffic service that I personally myself have used.

How to Promote Affiliate products for free?

One of the key characteristics of the latest internet-based affiliate marketing is having your own website or blog which is where you create content that is related to the product that you intend to market.

If your website is properly formatted, different search engines will provide visitors to your website at no cost to those looking for the products or services you're advertising. This technique is known in the field of search engine optimization (Website positioning) which is an easy method to promote additional affiliate products.

Optimizing Your Content

Content is the primary factor that drives results from search engines. The words on a website and web pages are a signal to search engines which is similar to Google and what it's all about.

When people conduct a search for a specific topic such as canine obedience training, Google delivers search engine results pages (SERPs) using the information that their algorithm (or algorithm) decides are the most relevant pages. There are a variety of ways to improve the quality of your content to rank it higher and you also receive free traffic. The first step is to make use of key words.

Keywords

Keywords are words that may be related to your field of expertise or subject. These are the types of terms potential customers will use when searching on the internet for the type of information and products you have to offer.

The title, the evaluation, or the article's title must contain at minimum one key word. The content should contain that key word and at least three other key words. The key phrases combined provide what's called semantic help that helps define what the website's content is about.

Many entrepreneurs try to "stuff" key phrases, using them over and over again; However, Google will penalize you for doing this. It is recommended to write with a natural voice, the way you would for an individual , not just the search engine.

Keyword Your File Names

Use key phrases in all of your file names, reminiscent of crucial phrase.HTML,.php,.jpg,.mp4, and so forth. These records could be located through Google and may lead to several items in the SERPs.

Links to Your Site

Links from popular websites such as social media sites can give you with a tiny website ranking boost.

Keywording Links

When creating the link that will take you to the affiliate website page, you should not just use the phrase "click here." Make use of key words that provide important information regarding the product.

Brand Names and Product Names

Make sure to use of these words as well. There are a lot of partners selling products on the market. It's true, however, having optimized content will put your company ahead of other competitors.

Chapter 7: YouTube

The growth of YouTube influencer is a phenomenon that should not be ignored. As of 2017 YouTube had more than 1,300 million users. Spend a few minutes absorbing this staggering number and imagine the amount you would earn if you could persuade a tiny part of the users to buy the items you're promoting. Some YouTubers earn thousands of dollars in earnings, there's plenty of room for anyone who would like to grab an ounce part of that pie. It is important to realize that YouTubers that earn an impressive amount of money do not only affiliates. Many have earned big money by partnering with brands to pay for ads and also monetizing their channels so that they earn money by the number of views they receive.

Making an account on a YouTube channel is simple and cost-free. It is necessary to have an account on Google account before you can sign to YouTube. Once you have signed in to YouTube then click"Create Channel" or click on the "Create Channel" button located in YouTube "Settings". Although creating a channel is easy and straightforward, gaining followers can be more challenging. You can win over fans and subscribers by creating unique video content that people will love. In contrast to written content, that you can hire writers and then copy and paste the final content demands more authenticity. Your viewers will be able to observe your facial expressions and be able to tell if you're clueless of what you're selling.

The benefit of YouTube for reviews of products or affiliate advertising is that it allows you to show your viewers visually how the product works. It's not a problem to describe how a specific product for moisturizing your face performs. Even with the most eloquent adjectives, you could not be able to capture the efficacy of the mask. With videos, there is an unquestionable proof of its effectiveness, and your viewers will be more likely buy the mask on their own.

Setting up Your YouTube Account

You can sign up to YouTube with your email account at work or a Gmail address. It is also possible to use an existing Google+ account to tie into YouTube. YouTube page.

Log in or sign up to get an account on YouTube. YouTube account.

Choose the gear symbol.

You'll see "see all my channels" or you may choose to start a new channel.

If you choose to an option to create a channel, you'll be asked to name the channel. You can make the channel's name your business name.

Choose a brand or product that is most appropriate for your business segment.

I agree with the conditions.

The channel will be able to display tabs for home and about, videos playlists, channels and discussions. You can also include special channels.

Click on the About tab to start filling in your profile. Fill in an explanation of your purpose, brand's message or tagline to describe the channel. It should be a compelling statement.

Link to other social media sites on the web.

Select a profile picture that best suits your business.

Include channels you are already enjoying Find new channels and then share channels. When you add channels, they could originate from your partner companies, or other departments within your company as well as individual employees or even companies that have content relevant for your products or services.

Creator Studio is the place where you'll control your contents.

The community is similar to all online communities in the sense that you must keep it in check and manage it. Your visitors can join you with this community

and ask for help and even share their thoughts.

YouTube Tips

Upload quality videos if you have content that is relevant.

Link to other profiles as well as other channels.

Upload videos that are interesting and informative.

Keep your community running smoothly and organized. Always answer questions, get rid of spam and ensure that your members have a great time on the channel.

Analyze your audience using analytics to determine demographics as well as playback locations and traffic sources, as well as the retention of your audience, and the devices used to view content. These pieces of data can help you create content that keeps your targeted viewers interested.

Create or share the videos you want to share that have relevance. For instance, for example, if you're selling vacuums, you should have an explanation of the way it operates and add humor or even entertainment. Would you want to watch an hour-long video on how to troubleshoot the vacuum? Maybe, if your company sold vacuums, but the majority of people wouldn't. They'd be watching the vacuum move around taking care of the floor, especially when you have cats who is riding on it.

Chapter 8: Create Your Profit Machine

Once you have received your Affiliate Link, you are able to now begin creating your own video to upload to Your YouTube Channel.

I'll show you step-by-step how to make videos without having to film yourself or creating the video from scratch!

In addition, if you already have an existing YouTube Channel, that's great!

If not, refer to the step-by-step guide for novices below:

(https://youtu.be/b38ef8n1p4U)

YouTube is the second most popular search engine, second only to Google which is why it is extremely profitable to utilize it for promoting products or affiliate deals. The best part is that it's completely free! You won't have to pay for ads for the rest of your life.

Everyone is on YouTube every day. You are able to enjoy a steady flow of targeted traffic for free all day long. Make sure to upload helpful and quality videos on a regular basis.

Millions of videos have been shared and uploaded via the platform and there appear to be no sign to slowing.

It will only get bigger as because more and more people realize the value in video-based marketing.

Our system can make use of its ability to upload videos that have an affiliate hyperlink embedded within the description of the video.

The Secret Source

Utilizing videos under the Creative Commons license, we can discover videos without copyright problems.

Creative commons licenses offer a common way for creators of content to grant another person permission to use their work.

YouTube lets creators label their videos with Creative Commons.

You can visit YouTube and look up your keyword/s.

In our case we're making use of "make money online" keywords.

Enter "make money online" and then click "Filter".

Select "Creative Commons":

It will provide you with all the videos that can repost on your channel on YouTube. Pick one that is interesting to you with lots of views.

We will then use it to market our product.

Let's select any video that is available. Ideal is around 10 minutes. This is just enough for our needs.

Then, click on the video and then copy the URL just above the search box.

We are going to download this video and upload to our own site using a free online video converter/downloader.

To do this, visit en.savefrom.net. Copy and paste the YouTube link in the above paragraph and it will begin download of your YouTube video.

Click"Download" and press the "Download" button and it will be downloaded automatically to your personal computer.

After you have the video in the computer you are using, recommend that you create your own thumbnail of the video prior to uploading it on your website channel. This makes your video distinctive and exciting for viewers.

To create a basic thumbnail, visit canva.com and create a no-cost account.

It's an amazing site that lets you design different styles for all your social media posts for free. Naturally, should need more features, can simply sign up for their Premium and PRO membership.

You can use it for free for the rest of your life. :)

If you want to learn how to use Canva, go to (https://youtu.be/XqYti78riU8) It will show you how to design almost anything in a nutshell using Canva.

I've used this website for quite a while I would strongly recommend it.

After you've completed your thumbnail, you're now ready to post your video on your channel on YouTube.

Just in case it is your first time to upload videos, go to

(https://youtu.be/h1lcSVnE4Ok) for the step by step instructions.

After uploading your video and the thumbnail, you must come up with a catchy subtitle and description.

Utilize the keywords we mentioned in the past for the title "How to make money online in 2019".

Take a look at videos that have high ratings with lots of views. take the title and model it and the tags on the video from it.

Write a compelling description

Your description must contain your keywords. This is essential to SEO (Search Engine Optimization). This will help you rank your videos.

This is the place where we intend to put the affiliate link!

When people view your videos, they'll read their description before clicking on your link, and they'll be taken onto the sale page for the offer, and they purchase the item and boom! You earn easy commissions, without having to do anything.

It's passive income that runs in autopilot. There isn't a single job on earth which gives you this freedom. That's why I am a fan of affiliate marketing. It's easy to set up and it'll earn you with a steady income for many the years to come.

The best part is that the potential for income is unlimited! Sky can be the only limit.

Just do the work first and, after that, you'll be able to put it aside. You can then wash and repeat the process.

The video description should include specific information about the offer you're trying to promote and any other deals you might have. Take a look at the following sample:

You can include any affiliate links you would like in one video that you upload. Don't go overboard. You can use the format above If you'd like or simply develop your own style.

The reason is that you're offering value to viewers and solving their problems with your videos. At the at the same time, using the platform to promote your products and services, and making money.

VERY IMPORTANT TIP:

Only promote items that you'll purchase for yourself. Do not promote items that is fraudulent or has little or no worth. If you provide value, customers will definitely return and be loyal to you.

Don't be tempted to promote everything you see on the internet. Be careful and make sure that the product is offered by an established seller.

The quality of your work is the most important factor when you are looking to earn an enormous amount of money.

Getting Traffic

You must now advertise this video via your social media platforms to receive that first remark. Spread the link to everyone you can to spread the word and make it go viral.

Create accounts on Instagram, Facebook, Pinterest and Twitter. All of them are completely free. I'm sure that you already have them all. If not, it's extremely easy to design one.

When the video is successful in the rankings there is no need to take any action.

It's already a free source of traffic. Make sure to select videos that are beneficial for your viewers.

This is the strength of this system.

You can repeat the process, and then create additional videos on a regular basis not only in the wealth but in various categories like relationships, health and other.

Clickbank has a wide variety of offers that cover all the major three categories. Choose the one with excellent commissions and high-quality deals.

Chapter 9: Turning Affiliate Marketing Into A Passive Income

Growing and sustaining your Affiliate Business

Your job being an affiliate marketing professional doesn't stop with having a great website and promoting goods and services offered by merchants. You have to complete certain tasks periodically These include;

Watch out for errors on your site or online store

Your website is more than a marketing, it is time to utilize plugins available from WordPress which can assist you set up an online stores. If you are looking to create an online store , then you must check out the website which is being used by the sellers who sell the products and services that you are promoting. Check for glitches in the technical system of those online stores as they could result in a loss of sales.

One of the most common ways to lose potential leads and customers is when you have constant technical problems on your websiteVisitors will surely prefer to go to a different site. It is essential to consider using affiliate websites which have an online store in order to make sure that your customers who have been referred can purchase items easily and directly through them.

Be sure to check the price of the product that you're selling

Traffic to your site is a great benefit for you, but it is important to make sure that your links aren't damaged and are efficient in directing visitors to your affiliate site. Be sure to have every product properly described with the appropriate article as well as keywords, and make sure the product's features are prominently highlighted. Additionally the price of the product must reflect of the price on the market. Experts advise that affiliate marketers aim towards products that fall within the 10 to 100dollar price range, since products that are priced higher may earn more commissions, but they do not easily sell as cheap products.

Make sure you're involved in affiliate marketing to be successful

If you do not add the latest affiliate links and content to your site What can you do to get to attract more people to join your list of followers and make revenue for your business? It is not necessary to create daily new content however, you must ensure that you are consistent with your postings regardless of whether you choose to update your content on a regular basis. Ensure that your content is shared across all social media channels and ensure affiliate links are present on every website page. When visitors want to see more of your content They simply want to return to your site as often as they like. If your website's content doesn't match the product that you're advertising, it may be the cause of concern. Therefore, you need to find the best product or similar to the content you have. Always look for the closest possible match to your website content.

* Make each one of your guests count.

Don't make a distinction between your visitors, with the reason is that you do not know who could generate prospects for your business. It is your responsibility to try the best you can to acquire their contact information every when they react to your content or to the item you are selling on your site. Do your best to experiment with all the affiliate products you can. Make sure you test them and if they're successful you can put them on your site. Be sure to review any products that are not worth your time and eliminate them from your site prior to them harming your reputation.

When you collect your customers contacts and you want to contact them regularly, particularly when they've purchased through your website, which means that you should never let your visitors to leave empty handed You can also offer them a web-based content for free that offers additional information (how to make use of the product, for example). Information is a great gift that for your customers to access). A few potential buyers should be reminded on a regular basis of the value of a product to persuade them to make an purchase. Repetition with potential customers will eventually provide them with an incentive to buy an affiliate item.

*Make sure to make sure you sell to the appropriate individuals

A lot of affiliate marketing novices may be wondering who exactly they should target. It is likely that you want to sell to anyone you can however, you must be aware of this. If your site's content contains instructions on how to create websites, for example an common person who doesn't know how to create websites will view it as valuable information however a computer geek might see it as amateur website. Do your best to convince beginners and novices by your writings and don't debate with experts too much, even if they leave negative feedbacks about your web content. You can try to delete any negative feedbacks.

Be sure that any old pages that do not generate sales is removed, while the ones that generate traffic are constantly refreshed with new content.

*Review your affiliate marketing strategies

Your marketing strategy at times should be reviewed if you truly intend to turn affiliate marketing into an ongoing passive income source. At some points it is necessary to carry out an review the strategies you use to market your affiliate. You must examine everything from the beginning until the last moment, and these include:

Your web design,

Strategies for optimizing your search engine (SEO),

The placement of your affiliate link, and

Your social media strategies.

The design of your website is as crucial as any other method of promoting your website. Your site must be easy to navigate that means the time it takes for your site to load after visitors arrive it should be rapid. Websites that load slowly can be a deterrent and visitors will seek out a different site and this means that you'll be losing a substantial portion of affiliate revenue. Check the speed at which visitors can access your website from time the time, and update or upgrade the website that isn't loading speedily immediately.

Your SEO strategies are crucial. Take the time to create outbound and inbound links, particularly from trustworthy websites. Links from outbound and inbound are effective to redirect more visitors through other sites to your site. Other strategies, such as keyword optimization are crucial since they assist visitors in locating your website quickly.

The placement of your affiliate links must be judicious. In particular, you should not use these links too much to the in the sense that there are numerous banners on your home page, creating a barrier for your viewers to appreciate your content. The banners of affiliates should be only used sparingly.

Be sure that your social media profiles are constantly updated, and include new followers, and keep providing them with information which can be beneficial to them. You must be constant with your updates, and don't hesitate to respond to their questions or comments.

Consistency is the main ingredient to being a successful affiliate marketing professional. It's not necessary to devote long hours. But taking at least an hour a day, the development of your affiliate marketing strategy. is sure to have an enormous impact on the long-term success of your business.

Chapter 10: How To Use Paid Advertising To Make Money Faster?

One of the initial problems that every affiliate marketer will confront is whether they should go for paid traffic or stick on free visitors. Free traffic can be appealing due to the fact that they're cost-free, but over the long term it is not going to allow you to reach an even larger audience, especially due to the new algorithmic trends that are coming into the market. There are many content creators across the globe and everybody is trying in one way or another to make money from their content. If you are confined to traffic that is free it could be several years before you see any significant increase in traffic.

For free traffic, you'll need to have excellent SEO skills and this is something you'll be able to use in your business. However, a bit of paid advertising is never a bad thing.

Therefore, before we dig into the specifics of how to use paid advertisements, it is important to understand the benefits of this process so you're motivated to making use of it in the affiliate marketing company you run.

So, here are some of the advantages you can get by utilizing paid advertisements These are just a few of the benefits you can enjoy from paid advertising

Growth faster - As mentioned the free traffic is great however if you wish to move up the ladder of growth quicker paying for advertising will bring you benefits in this sense. If you're still skeptical, take a look at your competition and make a analysis with other websites within the same industry. Compare who has a higher domain authority when compared to yours and finding the right one will be easier. Finding continuous free traffic can be a difficult procedure , particularly due to the variables that influence the process. So when you master the art of paying for advertisements, you can build your foundation more quickly.

Why should you wait around for years to make profit from your affiliate marketing efforts immediately? When you begin optimizing your efforts your growth, it will be noticed quickly and PPC advertising or pay-per click advertising is the best way to get the right target audience. Your posts will rank higher than they did before when you employ the correct strategies for paid advertising.

Increased targeted reach - If you rely solely on SEO strategies in your process of growth however, you might not reach the correct audience or even that you are not reaching the correct intended audience. So, you might not be attracting the correct kind of customers who will actually purchase something. Let's take this as an illustration. There is a blog post on a particular brand of shoes for which has affiliate links. When you publish your blog post, you'll receive visits and traffic from different sources, and also organic Google search results as well. Does this sound like a dream? It is, until one day you realize all the traffic you've generated isn't serving you well since these customers aren't actually buying anything. The main goal for affiliate marketing is have people click the affiliate link and purchase the item or service. So, what could have gone wrong? It's simple that the audience was not targeted. When traffic was natural but not organized and unspecific. To achieve success your ideal audience perhaps men who belong to the age range of 20-30 who are looking to run. That's why you need to be specifically targeted and paid advertising will allow you to reach this kind of reader. This won't just bring visitors, but will also convert your readers into loyal followers of your blog if the content is captivating enough. The most appealing aspect is that this can be done in an extremely short period of time by using paid advertisements.

Make your website's traffic sales. The process of writing a blog post does not necessarily take a lot of time when compared with the amount of time you'll need to invest in the creation and promotion of the blog post. You must have heard, time is money, so don't spend it on something that isn't going to yield results. So, what's the best solution? First you can engage the results of your paid advertisements. This is due to the fact that all the testing and experimentation that you conduct to create your affiliate marketing business work takes a lot of time-consuming, so should you not try to make the most out of the time you have?

If you are relying on SEO for all you do, it could be a long time before you make a substantial income. You'll spend the months working to be visible in the world's eyes particularly with this number of competitors to compete with.

In contrast If you opt for paid advertisements, you are sending your content to specific people who could have an interest in purchasing the item. In simpler terms paying for advertising can increase your conversion rate, that is directly related to increased sales.

It isn't necessary to make much investment. One of the biggest myths about paid advertisements is that it's expensive. It isn't! All you require is some dollars to start with the paid ads that are found on all social media platforms. With this little amount you can begin focusing on certain groups of people and test if it will work for you. After a couple of such hits and test experiments in advertisements, you'll be able to recognize which audience is worth investing your money into because they'll earn you a good profit. If you're just beginning, you should try split-testing. That means you'll need to split your marketing budget in different advertising campaigns. Then, at time, say after a particular period of time, for example 15 days, you can analyze which one of the campaigns performs the most efficiently. This will make the process of converting your target audience to leads. To give you an idea, a budget of $10 can be enough for a single entrepreneur to put into their ad campaign each week and will yield decent profits.

After you have learned about the many benefits that advertising paid for can bring, it's time to figure out how to go about it. In the beginning there are some best practices that you must be aware of in order to understand the fundamentals of paid advertising in relation to the creation of content in affiliate marketing.

Tip 1 Make sure you are targeting the right people

This is a point that has been reaffirmed repeatedly in different chapters, and with good reason since your audience is everything. Affiliate marketing is only driven by the amount of traffic and the conversion rate. The first step in paid advertising is to determine the ideal customers for your business. Ad targeting isn't a huge number of steps, and therefore many people hurry through the process to cut time. But , this isn't the right time to be thinking about how much time you're investing in it since this is the most crucial factor that determines the success of your company. It is important to spend the time as you can to pinpoint precisely the people who would be interested in purchasing the product you're selling.

It is possible that you are running an amazing advertisement, but not earning enough. This is often the situation for people who don't invest enough time to target. You may need to invest hours exploring the different target groups and whether they yield results or not. However, if you feel there is something wrong do not put off making adjustments and tweaks to your target audience since this is precisely what you have to make until there's a perfect match.

However, if you're nervous to tackle all this on your own or you simply don't have time to conduct all the necessary research to market, you could put aside money for the hiring of an expert consultant in this subject. This way, you will be able to determine the most efficient ways to target your marketing more efficiently.

Tip 2 - Conduct an exhaustive keyword analysis

The keywords you choose to use in your ads play a significant part in shaping the overall picture. They're the ones that present your content and present it to the public and, if they aren't correct by themselves, your message will be delivering to the wrong people. This becomes more crucial when dealing with a platform such as Google AdWords.

So, how do you determine the appropriate keywords to use in your content? Begin by brainstorming all the keywords that your readers could use to search for relevant content. Consider yourself in the shoes as a consumer and think of what you might have used as a key word to find the information you're searching for. These are the keywords that are identified as 'niche terms because of they are directly related to your particular niche. Also, you must ensure that the keywords you use correspond to the content's topic.

The auto-complete bar in Google is yet another fantastic method to find relevant keywords to incorporate into your marketing campaigns. By doing this you will get a variety of versions of the same topic. Additionally, you'll get the words in the order that are the most searched for. Try various keywords and changing them, which leads us to the final aspect of this subject...

Tip 3: Keep the testing going and make adjustments as needed.

This aspect is so crucial that it merits an additional mention. Therefore, don't stop trying until you see the results you've been hoping for, because if you're not seeing results, the issue lies in your strategy and not in anything else. Optimizing and continuous improvement are the keys to the success of an ad campaign and you shouldn't forget this.

Apart from these suggestions don't stress about getting it right in the first go-round since it's not going to happen that way. There will be some pitfalls, but the most important thing is to keep trying.

However, you will also need to choose the platform you will run your advertisements. The platform you choose should be suitable to promote the product(s) that you write about and should be able to reach the audience you want to target. Test and all is good but to make sure that you're making an informed choice we've compiled some of the most effective paid traffic sources commonly used by affiliate marketing and why they are beneficial to you.

Google AdWords

It's nothing more than the paid-for advertising platform offered by Google. If you conduct a search on Google it is likely to see a few advertisements on the top. These are posts that have been advertised that are displayed on the top of results, and this is before the organically-listed websites are placed in a ranking. What kind of advertising aimed at? It is important to be aware that of all the searches on the internet 77% is handled by Google. This means that almost every person or business can benefit from and use Google AdWords in their business.

This is the power of this platform. Consider this in this way What are you doing when you need to purchase something? You do a search on Google isn't it? This is the same thing your readers do too. People trust Google to deliver them the correct results. Hence that creates Google among the top advertising platforms as people are likely to visit Google to seek answers to their questions about purchasing decisions and products addressed. It is essential to have your blog posts up to date for all the questions you might have.

Facebook Ads

Of all the different social media sites, Facebook currently stands to as the most popular. They also have the biggest advertising platform for social media. The various parameters utilized by Facebook to improve their ads ability to target users are impressive. Additionally, they update their capabilities from time to time to provide you with a better advertising experience. The current count in active Facebook users Facebook stands at 2.2 billion. This is astonishment, but it's real. Therefore, you'll definitely reach your people on Facebook. What you need be doing is to make use of the numerous options Facebook provides and create an ad campaign that gives you optimal outcomes. Another fantastic feature you can avail with Facebook ads is Retargeting. It is possible to retarget your audience. Facebook Pixel is a feature which can be added to your website , and this will allow you to draw users who have previously been to your website before. The concept behind this feature is that time and effort needed to convert a regular user is smaller than the effort required to convert a new user.

Instagram Ads

Since Instagram is controlled by Facebook and Facebook and has gone through numerous major changes in the last couple of years, most notably its Instagram Live and Instagram Stories. The principle of Instagram is to create an all-purpose platform that can be used for visually appealing things. The best aspect is that there are more than 600 million users using Instagram, a photo-sharing application where you can also share videos specifically thanks to IGTV which has brought an entirely new world. You can decide on the goals for advertisements based on your requirements. You may run ads to increase engagement, or make it a goal of generating paid traffic. What is the best time to be using Instagram over Facebook? The answer isn't easy. If the product that you offer on your affiliate marketing blog are visually appealing, and your target viewers are mostly young and young people, then Instagram is a great place to try out your ad campaigns as a novice.

However, regardless of the traffic source you decide to use it is important to be aware of check their regulations and restrictions because all of them have restrictions. If you don't pay attention to those restrictions and advertising almost everything could lead to warnings and the permanent closing of your account, and you certainly wouldn't want to do that. These restrictions generally revolve around misleading banners that are designed to attract attention but they don't make any real assurances. Additionally, you won't be able promote all kinds of content through any popular advertising network, such as for any sexually explicit or sensitive content.

Also, you must ensure the high-quality traffic. The most significant issue that plagues every kind on social networks is the massive quantity of bots. It is also referred to as fake traffic. However, you should not fall into the trap of fraud and remind yourself that your reputation as a business is the most important thing. Therefore, you must be wary of such practices and play with legitimate traffic only. Conduct extensive research on all the issues covered in this chapter, and do not leave a stone to be left unturned. If you adhere to the steps listed above, you'll be successful distant.

Chapter 11: Become An Authority

As a novice affiliate marketer the most difficult obstacle you will have to conquer is providing your potential customers a reason to believe in you, as opposed to the many other options which are easily accessible online. Although not the most straightforward route, the most effective approach to conquer this challenge and propel your site to the top of results of search engines simultaneously, is to establish yourself as an expert in your chosen field.

In many cases the words expert and authority are frequently used interchangeably but this isn't the case in sales however, because having authority is the most important thing as being an authority is more than just getting a second position. In this context an expert is someone who has a vast knowledge of specific areas of expertise, and being an authority refers to the one who all the expert agrees is your primary destination for information. In other words authorities aren't experts just because they say they are but they are experts since when they announce their position about their subject of interest, others take note of them.

The advantages from being an authority in your chosen field are similar to being an authority in any other circumstance. in which you speak, people will listen. The reason is that people who are aware that you're an authority will naturally to believe you know the subject matter you're talking about in the particular context. It's not difficult to realize how this could be translated into more conversions, if you give it a little additional boost. If you can achieve the level of authority in your field in the future, you'll be capable of setting the tone for your niche overall, with a plethora of followers who will automatically accept whatever you have to make clear.

If it appears that you're giving niche experts excessive credit for their work, think about the person you consider as an authority within your field of preference. It is more likely than the average of listening to what they have to say on everything and likely to do not give much thought to the process when doing this. It's not to say that you're not right since you put your trust in this person due to reasons, but it illustrates the power such people enjoy.

It begins with research: The very first step in becoming an authority in your chosen field will be the most challenging by the end of the day and there aren't any shortcuts to follow. In essence, if you'd like to be regarded as an authority, you must learn all about the subject that you will proclaim to have authority on. Since even the tiniest topic can be wide, to avoid having to learn about every in your field Do yourself a favor choose a niche instead.

This will not only save you hours of research but it will also allow you to not directly challenge the authority of other experts who may already be in the field.

When you're ready to work, it's essential to go beyond just acquainting yourself with the Wikipedia page on the subject This means visiting the other sources you discover that are connected to the Wikipedia page and tracking the sources that are listed there as well. Then, you'll want to repeat the process repeatedly until you can declare that you've done everything you can to make sure that there is no gap left. It will require plenty of effort and hard work but the end results will definitely pay off in the end.

While going through the procedure, you might consider putting an introduction to the subject as if you were writing for someone who is completely new to the particular subject you're focusing on. When writing a book on something you're still learning about may appear like placing the cart ahead of the horse, but the reality is that thinking about the methods to simplify complicated subjects into their simplest elements will allow you to consolidate what you've learned and make sure that you're able to write with ease on the subject in the near future. The aim is not to simply rehash well-known facts, but to provide a thought-provoking debate to the subject of interest. The ability to bring up the types of questions that people in the industry is asking is an excellent method to ensure that you are on the right path.

Think about your voice: Each writer has a distinct voice, one of an era perspective of the world, which is evident in their choice of words and the way they express themselves. In a highly intense online market, honeing your voice could be the distinction between being an expert and just another persona-less expert. Your voice is what differentiates your content from the rest, so make every effort to make sure it's as unique and as captivating as is possible. If you're not sure about is the best voice for your needs is, take a look at the following.

The most effective way to begin is to create an outline of all the words you think others might use to describe your personality. Spend some time with each one of them and consider ways to create each one as concise as possible in regards to expressing your personality through your writing. Then, you might be able to incorporate the equivalent written version of any distinctive speech patterns you may have. They aren't easy to figure out on your own so you're likely to require outside help to achieve the most effective outcomes. It is possible to express these kinds of things, including the structure of the sentences you choose to use, the manner in which you divide your paragraphs and how long your paragraphs are, and more. It's okay when you're unable to find a way to express your thoughts in the present, but the longer you write and the more unique your writing will eventually develop.

If you aren't able to find an initial voice it's important to let it grow naturally, rather than pushing it. A voice that is forced is likely to hinder your voice's development and will ultimately paint you in a corner. when you alter your voice after the people are used to it , you be in danger of losing their trust.

Make sure that your readers know the content you're reading: While you are working to establish your credibility on your subject, it's essential to recognize that you'll never know all there is to know about your field. At some point you will be able to get to identify who the top name names in the industry are, and you'll want to show that you're getting your information from credible sources. This will let them know that you are able to distinguish good sources from those that aren't and adds to your authority overall.

Before sharing the source of the data you're using, it's essential to scrutinize them thoroughly to make sure that everything is as authentic as it appears. This includes being aware of who wrote the information you plan on referencing , along with the level of authority they have in the particular field. The credibility of reliable sources can be easily verified, and you'll be able to conduct thorough research on the names you're referring to in order to make sure they don't have any hidden skeletons in their closets. While it may appear to be an overwhelming task however, it'll be worth it if it keeps the possibility of making a big error and causing yourself to be an unpopular social stigma.

Spread the word After you've acquired all the information you need you need to learn about the specific segment of the topic What you'll want to do is disseminate the knowledge you've learned to as many people as you can. In order to do this it is going to be able to spend time on other websites you know are popular with your targeted group, particularly those with active forums. You may be required to join a regular posting on the subreddit that is devoted to your topic.

At this point you'll be able to fully be absorbed in the field Begin to have conversations with other people, address questions and generally present yourself in a positive manner. When you post a blog you'll need to link your knowledge to your website so that your audience can go anywhere and not see your face or the name of your website. When doing this it is crucial to stay clear of any affiliate posts to these sites, which will be added later. Everything is concentrated on creating an unifying movement around the concept of your knowledge.

If you are trying to make your name known on the internet, it is crucial to go beyond speak about the basics of the field, although answering any questions that people may have is acceptable. In fact, you're going be looking to utilize your blog posts as a chance to demonstrate your expertise by going over and above what the members of your target market might have a basic understanding of because they're interested in their area of expertise. By moving the conversation in different ways will people remember your name following reading your article.

When your name is being mentioned by people who are in your field The next thing you're going to need to accomplish is to take your status to the next level by making contact with other experts in your field by extending a friendship offer. Develop a relationship with them before proposing to guest post on their blog for them for a week, if they are worried about not meeting an important deadline. You'll be aware at this point, generating adequate content for your site to stay online and running all the time can be a daunting task and they're likely be very grateful to help.

While helping the competition may seem like the last thing you would want to be doing, when in fact you will get more value from this process than the effort you put into. In the first place, it puts your site and your name exposed to a large new audience, so it's a certain way to increase conversions from people who click through to your website in the process. However it will demonstrate to your people who read your blog that the individual they trust trusts them enough to allow you to post an article to your website, thus making your blog more authoritative. If you are able to convince this to cooperate with a large majority of other experts within the field and it appears as if they're all bowing to you, and give your blog the look of authority in no time at all.

Your aim in these situations isn't to make a single conversion although that's always good, but rather to attract followers who believe that you're the end all be all the authority of your niche or sub-niche. Your pockets will be filled with conversions however, your followers are likely to make a point to share the news with their friends about your brand and attempt to persuade them to browse your blog and, in turn the affiliate products you offer. Even if they don't buy something, they are going to add value to your worth in terms of conversions. They must be carefully nurtured to ensure that they stay as passionate as is possible.

Create an article or book

If you've completed all the required research You should have enough information to write an ebook about your subject that ranges approximately 8 to 15 thousand words. If you feel that's too much, think about the guide to help you write during your research phase. You can think about it as a comprehensive outline of what you could incorporate into your ebook. It's a daunting idea however, if you look at the amount of writing you've done for different blogs, you'll realize that the number of words is much less daunting than it may have appeared.

If you're not in the mood or the desire to write a novel of your own, employ a freelance ghostwriter at a cost of around 1 cent per 100 words. That allows you to write a book of 10,000 words for less than $100 due to marketplaces for freelancers such as UpWork.com. Whatever you choose to do, you'll most likely need to engage an experienced graphic designer to design the covers for the front and back of your book, as having a professionally designed book can boost your credibility significantly. The cost will probably be about the same, or just a bit more than the cost of writing the book would cost.

The ultimate goal would be to publish the book you want to publish on the Kindle Marketplace, at no cost because Amazon will take a portion of the revenue, but you should give the publication on your website to those who sign to receive your newsletter since it is a powerful advertising tool. After the book is made available on Amazon You will need to ensure that you include prominently on your site , as there is no way to prove that you're an authority on a topic like creating a book about the subject.

Chapter 12: Available Networks

As I've mentioned before that the majority of new affiliate marketers should opt for an affiliate program that already exists and join it in order to begin selling items from a huge selection of items. The selection of specific affiliate programs might be a great option for more accomplished and established affiliates however, for those who are brand new to the field starting out, the best way to get started is by joining one of the networks. There are numerous affiliate networks and a lot offer the ability to sell your products on some of the most prominent websites for sales, offering you an enormous array of items you can begin selling immediately. Here are some examples of the most frequently used and top affiliate networks to provide you with a an overview of the different types of systems readily available today in the market.

Amazon Associates:

The name of the network suggests that this affiliate network lets you sell your products directly through one of the largest market places, Amazon. By joining the Amazon Associates will allow you to access millions of products , and also receive commissions whenever your customers go to Amazon through your affiliate links and buy products. Amazon Associates is one of the largest affiliate networks around the world, geared towards customers in the American market. When you join Amazon Associates, you can earn up to 10% of cost of sales, based on the type of product you sell. Having a an abundance of monthly sales can earn you more commissions.

eBay Partner Network:

Another excellent online retailer that offers an affiliate network available is eBay. Its eBay affiliate program is less popular than Amazon among affiliates but that could be the exact reason for you to take advantage of it rather than the Amazon Associates Program. The method eBay employs to determine the amount they will pay their members is complex and more sophisticated than the others affiliate network. If you're looking for simple methods, it isn't suitable for you. eBay Partner Network does, however, offer state of the art statistics and sales numbers are tracked and it is your decision whether you're happy with it or not.

ClickBank:

ClickBank is an enormous affiliate network that lets affiliates to select from a variety in digital products they can sell. These products comprise of self-help programs as well as money-making online schemes. A lot of these programs are excellent and are worth the cost to final customers. However, ClickBank does also get bombarded with fake plans as well as books, schemes, and schemes. Being an affiliate you'll have to decide which products you offer and what kind of branch you would like to have. Also, providing truthful reviews of products on your site with the potential for harm and providing your customers with options will help gain their trust and help you increase sales.

FlexOffers:

Another huge and powerful affiliate network that includes more than 500 advertisers from all kinds of industries and is FlexOffers. FlexOffers was recognized as among the most popular affiliate networks of 2015 and is among the top places to visit for those looking to start your journey into affiliate marketing.

Specialized Networks:

If you've decided to stick with one specific niche and decided to stick with the same one, you'll likely be able to locate an affiliate program specifically designed for your specific niche. If that's your situation, you may be interested in joining this network because it can offer greater commissions on sales as well as more precise statistics on the specific niche, and more support for marketers in the segment. Utilizing special network affiliates is something I highly recommend, but like with specific affiliate programs, this might be something that should be reserved for more knowledgeable marketers. Rather, making use of those Amazon as well as eBay network to begin with is definitely the best option.

The working details of an affiliate marketing program

* The different processes and steps that are included in Affiliate programs can be described below for information:

When you become an affiliate, you sign up first with the advertiser via the affiliate networks or direct. Once the contract has been signed and signed, you will receive an affiliate's specific URL or link with the affiliate's ID/username.

* You can then utilize this link to display on your site. Sometimes, an advertiser will provide you with banners or content that will appear on your website. These are usually an element of the agreement.

* If a user of your site clicks the advertisement's link an advertisement advertising cookie gets placed on the computer of the visitor.

* The user decides to purchase or performs a transaction through the advertiser's link.

If the customer completes the transaction the advertiser will then check the cookies on the computer and locate the affiliate ID of yours and grant credit for the purchase.

* The advertiser will then update the relevant reports to include visitor information and the sales your affiliate link's produced.

* Commission payments are paid regularly generally monthly, and are depending on the amount of lead and sales generated. They are stated in the contract agreement which is signed by both the publisher and the advertiser.

Nowthat you are aware and are aware of the concept of affiliate marketing and how it operates The next chapter will deal with the most commonly used terms within the world of affiliate marketing. This will let you determine what your contract's terms are, as well as how and when payments are made.

Chapter 13: Theme forest Affiliate Marketing With Example

Becoming an Affiliate

Each member can become affiliates by following the guidelines that are outlined in these guidelines. Be aware that if you would like to be active with the Affiliate Program, there are a few items you'll need in mind. These are outlined in the following paragraphs.

Recommend new customers to any on the Envato Market sites and you'll be paid a percentage from their initial cash payment or purchase!

Referral Code: Each member is automatically assigned a referral code, which is generated by using your username. The referral code can be found on the page for referrals.

Simply insert a link image button onto your website by using the code. If a user visits your referral link, and proceeds to open an account and buy something or deposit money via one among the Envato Market sites, you get a share of the first cash purchase or deposit.

Percentage of Referral Program: The percentage of earnings you can earn by taking part in the Affiliate Program are listed on the page for payments.

How the Affiliate Program Works

Set up an Envato Account and redirect traffic to any page of the Envato Market while adding your account username at after the address.

When a user who is new clicks your referral linkand registers for an account and buys an item (or makes a deposit) through any or the Envato Market sites, you get 30% of the first purchase price or cash deposit. If they put $20 into their account, you will receive $6. If they purchase an item worth $200, you receive $60.

Five Steps to Internet Marketing Success

Good quality content can is sure to attract followers, friends, and those that are interested in the offerings and services.

Customers who are interested in your products want to see what you're selling through pictures and sample. They'll also want to interact with you directly. Make the most of this opportunity to increase your reputation through Guest Blog Posts press releases, Infographics as well as Personal Blog posts and eBooks.

Guest Blog Post

Original Content

Innovative ideas and experiences

New Content boosts the quality of your Google Search Rankings

Make it important

Excellent spelling and grammar

Spelling can help you get higher rankings.

Easy to read

Some interesting headlines

Very well edited article that has been edited

Concise and clear

Make sure to use high quality images.

Be aware of the needs of your readers

Give information that is valuable to your readers

Authoritative website

Enhance the value of the web

Links, traffic of high quality, and the relevance

Create more trust

Do not be distracted

Too many ads, promotions or calls to action in the text

Posting YouTube Videos

Be sure to support what you're trying sell

Develop your credibility

141

Press Releases

Interesting content and useful information

Include the who, when, what and the reasons in advance

Write for the members of the media

Do you have something exciting to share?

Useful

Be imaginative

Make use of high-quality images.

Photos, videos, graphics

Improve brand recognition

Never include a testimonial

Share

Include contact information for the entire contact

Keep a record of press releases from your company.

Infographics

Information that is reliable and verified

Background information

Trustworthy

Relevant sources

Cite your sources

Tell an interesting story

Unique graphic design

Synthetize

Conceptualize

Branding interactions with customers

Synthetize

Conceptualize

A fascinating subject

Create something new

Share, distribute, and post

Personal Posts

Original content

Do share your own personal experiences

Expertise and personal information

To solve a problem, make it useful and relevant

Excellent spelling and grammar

Search engines reward writers with great writing skills

Be aware of the needs of your readers

Share the content

By sharing and interaction

E-Books

Define audience

Write to a certain target audience, with a specific subject

Original content

Relevant subjects

Interesting content

Make use of high-quality images.

Editorial design

Step-by-step instructions that are useful

Publish your work

Make sure to share your book on your social networks

Use blogs, email as well as your website's social media channels.

Offer value to win customers' respect and their attention

16 Tips for Success in Internet Marketing

Think Differently: Many people are taught by their schools and their parents to be competent employees. Learn the perspective of a business owner through books and expert advice. Along with reading, it is important to apply what you've learned.

Take Responsibility: You're accountable for the choices you make today in your life and not anyone else. What are you looking for? What must you accomplish to achieve it? Be determined and begin working towards it.

Benchmark: If people who have less resources are able to succeed, why shouldn't you? Prepare yourself to take on the long in the long run despite the obstacles. Take inspiration from other's achievements as an example of possible.

There is no compromise: People who are desperate tend to be more concerned with their own needs than they do about their customers and it's easily spotted. When you're not feeling desperate it's possible to take actions simply because it's the right choice to make.

Kaizen Continuously improve particularly in the way you think. Try to become VI-I an ever-growing g1 learner, constantly moving forward.

Do Less: A true business isn't about trading your time and effort for money. You should look for that 4% work that yields 64% of outcomes. Make sure you do what you'd like to do, the things that you can make a bigger impact, then delete and automate the remainder.

Stay with what works Use the winning strategies and get rid of the losers. Continue to do the actions that will yield the most effective outcomes.

Don't Give Up: If there is a clear indication that something isn't working, don't hesitate to give up. It's better to recognize that you're in error and try an alternative strategy.

Note: You don't have to figure out what is popular. Look at the things people want and require and what they're currently paying for. The answers are right in front of you.

Clarity The mind that is confused can't make a choice. Keep your customers' minds at ease whether it's the solutions you provide, your selling process, or the way you describe your solutions.

Own the RaceCourse: Create an official website that you own on which you place all your valuable content. Create a self-hosted site and on a speedy server, and with an address you control. Don't build your business using an external platform such as Facebook, Linkedin or YouTube.

Rich Content: Share content that addresses questions and solves issues. It can be in various formats, including audio, video images, text and make sure to do it frequently. Inform people via social media and email when you publish new material.

Results, Not Stuff: Less products, more value. It's not about the amount of products you are able to offer your customers, it's about getting the most effective results using the smallest amount of effort. This is particularly true for subscription services.

Create your own E-Mail Database: Your email list can be powerful. Make sure you have the right offer, ensure it is valuable and then deliver it at the appropriate time. Automate triggers, abandonment sequences , and solicitations for feedback.

However, you must keep your newsletters natural.

Unsubscribe from marketing emails. Don't let yourself be shackled to your email inbox. You are the one who is sending emails, not looking them up. Also, syndicate your emails to wherever people are for example, on Facebook, YouTube or Twitter.

Valuable Reach: If you're looking to make lots of money, make an enormous amount of value and get it before the most people you can.

Marketing Tips for Affiliate Products/Services

Find your target and check out Competitors

Which customers are targeted in your marketing efforts

Find your competitors. Examine and evaluate their marketing practices

Make a list of their top techniques

Optimize your website

Utilize specific keywords in headlines

Make sure your content is always fresh and distinctive

Make it easy for people to locate your contact details

Off Page Optimization

Include your website in the most popular Directories and place ads on websites that are popular with traffic

Enhance your backlinks with best blog sites and forums

Make high-quality videos which showcase your company's offerings and products. Advertise these videos on well-known sites such as Youtube.com

Update Content

Include a blog on your website to help educate your clients

Provide relevant information on your field on your blog's section

Social Media Marketing

Make a social community through Social Media sites

Create Relationships by through Social Media Interaction

Briefly describe Your Products and Services through Social Media Sites

Distribute relevant content via Social Media Sites even though there are times when the content was not developed by your team.

EMail Marketing

Create your Email subscriber list by using landing pages

Contact Customers via email when needed

Provide relevant information regarding Your Products and Services through Email Marketing

Tools you Need for Affiliate Marketing

1. Site Audit and Analysis

2. Keyword Analysis Tools

3. Keyword Rank Checker

4. Content Creation

5. Backlink Research Tools

6. Link Management Tools

7. Social Media Management and Analysis

8. Paid Advertising - Reporting and Analysis

9. Email Marketing

10. Affiliate Tools

11. Web/Lead Analytics - Reporting and Marketing

Survey Tools

Chapter 14: Fastest Way To Make $100 With Youtube

Did you know that YouTube is the very first video platform on the planet? and almost everyone is on YouTube each day, browsing and looking for information to help them resolve their problems.

Why not make use of this platform efficiently to bring visitors to our affiliate product. If you make use of youtube properly you can earn an incredible amounts of money each day and throughout the month. All you have to do is provide youtube what they want , and you'll begin to see a massive results.

It's important to note that I haven't yet tried this yet but I am planning to use this strategy starting this month, so I believe it would be great to include this strategy in this book so that you can test it just like I have been using this strategy for the year ahead.

My friend recently informed me about this method and how he is able to get an enormous amount of visitors to his affiliate product and making huge commissions in the long run.

So let do this together and please do not forget to shoot me a message at "davidnelsonofficial@gmail.com" if you get any result.

I enjoy hearing my testimonials from readers because they makes me feel good.

The requirement

This method will cost you not less than $30 to $50 to begin when you decide to outsource any tasks, but it will likely not cost you a cent in the event that you decide to tackle the task yourself.

Traffic! Traffic!! Traffic!!! Traffic !!!! !

We need traffic to be successful online, so we should make use of YouTube to deliver some fantastic targeted traffic to our affiliate site

To begin using youtube, follow these steps.

Log into YouTube and then create your own channel.

Click sign in and choose any Google email account to log into YouTube. Once log in

Click on the drop-down menu

Click on the setting

Click on the link to view all channels or create a brand new channel

Click the + New Channel to create a new YouTube business channel.

Enter the necessary information to name your channel and then verify your account. Then, click Done. This will create a brand new Account.

But do not !!!!! !

How do you name your channel?

It's a lovely idea that ought to be on your thoughts

This is where you need to think more strategically. It isn't enough to name your channel. You should choose the name you wish to rank for.

Assuming you're in the area of weight loss visit youtube and type the keyword into the search box

E.g. how do I lose weight quickly

In the drop-down menu, I am able to select ways to lose weight quickly on my YouTube channel.

This can narrow your channel and gives you the chance to rank quickly since when people search for that keywords, if the same name in the description, title of your video and the name of your channel share the same name. The chance of being ranked for the keyword is high.

Be sure to adhere to this advice because it's crucial and will make your video to perform better on YouTube.

Once you've decided on your area of expertise and have used the keyword you have chosen in creating your channel, then the second step is to upload video to your channel. You will then begin watching the results

You don't want to upload any video it is essential to have a professional video to be able to rank higher on YouTube

By following the method I am going to share within this ebook, you don't need to become an expert to or even in front of a camera , or even create a single video that you can upload to YouTube.

How To Create A High Quality Video For YouTube

Before you begin creating your video, must list 10 keywords you would like to rank for and then create a videos within those keywords.

For this,

Enter your keyword of interest into the YouTube search box, and you will get a list of keyword that drop down

E.g how to avoid losing (pics below)

You can now see a variety of keywords you can create videos around. If you click on an instance from the drop-down menu, you will be able to see an example of a keyword once you have your cursor over in the box for searching.

Ten keywords that you would like to make a video around

Let get started in create our video

There are two ways to go about this. The first is outsourcing the entire process , while the other is to handle it yourself.

Tools to Install

Before you begin searching for video content to create it is important to download this YouTube app known as "VID IQ" on your Google Chrome

The way this application works is, it gives you all the information about the video that is already ranking on YouTube in order to replicate the success of YouTube. I will go into more detail about this in the book. Once there is the movie downloaded to your browser, you can begin creating our video

Outsource

Assume that I would like to make an instructional video centered around "BEST EXERCISE TO LOSE WEIGTH FAST AT HOME". What I'll do is search for the keyword on YouTube and then look through the top 4 or 5 ranking videos on youtube. Copy and paste the link from YouTube video

The example below

What I'm going to do is to copy the URL of the video, and then go to rev.com. Click the transcription button and click on the start link.

Note. What we're trying to accomplish in this case is to collect the same words as were used in the video and then rewrite them as we don't want utilize some of the information to make an original video. We want to ensure that we're the legitimate owner of the video we created and there's no reason for us to believe that there's copyright issue.

The next step is to paste the YouTube URL link that you copied from YouTube and paste it into the link section.

What happens is that this site will automatically transcribe the video for you.

Be aware that this website costs $1 per minute. The longer the length of the video, the more money you will have to spend.

This video runs for 16 minutes. If I want to be able to get this transcript I'll be paying $16+ for the transcript.

After I have the transcript, I'm going to go to fiverr.com and click on the

Writing and transcription section

Enter copywriting into the search box.

Choose someone with an excellent job to write the transcript on your behalf or you can do it yourself.

This will force you to create an entirely new script to create your own video

The next thing to do once you have received an original version of your content by your ghostwriter is to should also consider hiring someone from Fiver to make the video for you.

To do this you need to hover your mouse

Animation and video section

Click on the SPOKE-PERSONS VIDEOS

Pick someone with a great record

After you have selected the person who will make the video on your behalf send this script script to whomever you have selected and ask them to create a professional-looking video for you.

Make sure you choose a an individual to create the video for you since it will make your video appear more professional.

Once you've got your video ready then you are able to publish the video on Youtube.

You can also forward the link to the producer and inform them that you require a particular video that is superior than the one that you send to them.

Title, Tag and Description Strategy

After you've completed your video and you are planning to share it through your own channel it is important to focus on tags and descriptions since they are among the elements that can aid in boosting your video's rank on YouTube.

Title

Choose the exact phrase you'd like to rank for in your title

Description

If you've got an existing video, you must replicate their success on YouTube. All you need to do is study the way they wrote their description and then copy exactly what they wrote. the only difference is to place your affiliate link at the front of the description, so that people is able to see your affiliate link without having to click the LEARN MORE link.

Don't copy someone else's description. Instead, study the method they describe their work and then do something similar.

Another thing to keep in mind is to use the keywords you wish to be ranked for at least twice in your description to boost your chances of being ranked since when Google looks at your description, title and the content of your video, they will move your video towards the top of the search results.

Tag

The tag is the one you'd like to devote your time. This will increase your success on YouTube however, you have everything you need to get done.

Did you know the tool you installed in your Chrome browser? "VID IQ" If not, you'll need to get it installed immediately

After you have installed it, you can scroll down to the video you'd like to copy their success and examine the tag they're using.

You'll want to use the same tag that you saw at their YouTube channel.

To locate this section, look to the right side of your screen while scrolling through the video. You will see the video tag. You can use the same tag for your video

You now have a video that's optimized for YouTube. Try this method and see if it works for you.

It is essential to continue posting videos on your channel to ensure that the channel is thriving.

If you do not have any money to invest, you can invest it yourself with the strategies in the following article.

Do it Yourself

By using this method you won't have to pay anyone else the only thing you need to do is to do is sit in your computer in create the video on your own.

You can go straight to the point.

The program we're going to employ to create our video will be called wave.video

The next step is going to the library, type in your keyword , or scroll down to locate your field of expertise.

As you can see, I've highlighted the fitness and sports area in the picture above. When I click on that section, I'll be able to see various types of videos I can make an extremely professional video. Another option is input the keyword directly into the search box and find the video you wish to utilize.

You can pick from the paid or free video. Both work great.

If you've found the video you wish to use, press the ADD button to make the video.

Based on the sample (youtube video) above, " best exercise to lose weight at home" We can combine up to seven or six exercise videos taken from wave.video.

For ideas on content for your next article, visit ezinearticles.com or Google

Enter your search term in the search box, and then see the magic happen.

Check out the image below.

You can now observe that ezine provides me with exactly what I wanted. What I'm going to do is click that link and begin putting the title of my video.

Search for any keyword , and add apply them in your movie. Take a look at the example image below.

Create a professional video. Since there's no voice in the video, you must incorporate a cool soundtrack to make your video look appealing to your viewers.

Another option is to make the video last longer than one or two minutes. A 2-minute video is acceptable.

After you have completed the process of making your video then the next step is hitting the publish button. Now your video is ready to upload.

Be aware that wave.video will put their watermarks on your video that won't make your video appear professional on YouTube. The only thing you have to do is follow a second step to get rid of the watermark on your video. It is as simple as subscribing for their monthly subscription to remove the watermark of your videos.

I suggest you opt for the business plan that allows you to create a video of 1 minute and up. You can opt for a either a monthly or an annual plan based on your requirements.

Wave.video subscription is worth the cost as you can make more professional videos that you can upload to Youtube and include free music in your video.

The most important thing to be successful on YouTube is uploading a professional video on youtube. Follow the procedure above (title tag, title description, and title) and you will see your video rank and get more views. When your video starts to rank and you have paid for wave.video subcroption is not difficult. All you have to do is do the work, and you'll be amazed by how this could alter everything

Now you have a professional-looking video that is ready to be published on YouTube. Upload your video to YouTube and click"Publish.

Continue to upload similar videos on your topic to YouTube. You can also add your affiliate link to earn income alongside.

Let's make some money in the year 2019 !!!! With a plan ......

Join us now to start making videos for your YouTube channel.

This is the method I'm going to use to earn money from affiliate products in 2019, so let's do it all together.

Important note: just create a the compilation with three to more (depending on the type of video you're creating) video, and you're finished.

If you are looking to take your on the internet with your business,, I suggest that you read the following chapter. You'll be amazed...

Chapter 15: Grow Your Business And Make Income.

To earn money at working from home and earning an income from home affiliate marketing is one of the most effective methods. To earn an income that is passive from affiliate marketing, it will take time and you'll have to put in lots of work. If you put in the right amount of work along with a business-minded outlook it is likely that you will achieve your goals.

Don't make the error of thinking that you only have to put ads on your site and sell products on your website and then begin to earn. Whatever good and attractive your website looks it won't earn profits until your visitors purchase it. To become an effective affiliate marketer, you must look after your business like a child. Consider your business to be a hobby and it will be paid for your time, but if you run your business as a business it will pay you like an enterprise.

It is not possible to be a millionaire overnight through affiliate marketing. However, if you've got the desire to put in time and effort, and most importantly , patience making money from affiliate marketing is very feasible.

Making A Commitment

You'll need to be committed to growing your business from scratch to become an effective affiliate marketer. If you're seeking a company with minimal investment and high return, advertising through affiliates is most effective. You only need to put in your time and energy into the growth of your company. This is the reason it is crucial to commit to your company.

You'll have to spend time researching your market and maintaining your websites as well as searching for for the products and services you wish to market. If you're consistently in all of these areas it will be easy to expand your business. It may not immediately pay off, but will certainly be worth it over time.

Staying Updated

The algorithm used by the internet is constantly changing and it can affect your business. For instance when there is an update to Google this could affect your position in the results of a search.

In this way, you need to keep up in the current changes that are happening to your business. You shouldn't simply update your site and forget about it. It is essential to keep up with the new changes and make the necessary changes so that you don't lose your website.

Sitting idle isn't going to help, you don't know when your website is going to go down.

Maintaining Your Site

It's crucial to keep your blog updated regularly. If you are using blogs to market products, then you need to be very active. You will need to make at least 2 articles per week. People who read blogs always want to read blog posts. If you don't deliver them, you could be unable to keep them.

You'll need to frequently make changes to the content of your website. It is essential to change the products that you're promoting on your website. Keep up-to-date with affiliate programs such as Amazon for example. Every when they release new products, ensure that you're the first to advertise the new product. This is the way to grow your company. Always offer something of value to your customers.

Achieving A Passive Income

Earning a passive income can be some time, perhaps even more. If you follow through with your plans and dedication you can create an effective affiliate marketing company. You'll need to put in your time and energy to achieve this. It will take quite a bit of time before you are able to finally relax and travel as the income roll into.

When you begin earning money from your business, then you can completely automatize your business. All you have to do is give orders, and let others do the work for you. It is possible to hire someone to manage your website or blog as well as all your social media accounts. It will take some time to get to that point. There's a saying " every CEO was once a worker" So, you must work hard and establish your empire first. You can then automate it to take whatever action you wish to make your income from passive sources. The level of your goal will determine the extent to which you're willing to go. Before showing up. You must establish the foundation and create an enterprise that is successful.

Chapter 16: List Building Secrets Marketers Don't Want You To Know

You're making a huge mistake in the event that you're not making an outline from the beginning. As sour as it may sound, you'll regret it in the future.

Lists are your goldmine. Internet marketers don't lie when they claim, "the money is in the list." List creating gives you the chance to keep in touch with a specific and interested segment of the population. The list you create is something that you have complete control over and influence over.

Google could make their next update, and remove the entire organic traffic you have in a matter of minutes. It's happened to many marketers. The followers you've earned through social media isn't yours to own. It's part of an online social media platform that can alter their policies and close your business before you are able to say Twitter. You're at best enlisting to use the social media websites to help build an audience.

In this unstable, unpredictable and ever-changing online environment Your list is an account you own. So, don't overlook the importance of creating a list or using email marketing with other types of advertising to create a loyal fan base.

It's not as cheesy as you think it is a great way to earn you money in a matter of minutes even while you're asleep. Once you have a database of potential customers who are who are interested in the products or services you're selling and you are able to make a variety of interesting opportunities. It is possible to promote everything from digital products as well as physical products, courses and membership sites through affiliate.

You can distribute exclusive offer flyers, newsletters and monthly updates promotions for new products Launch offers ebooks, free eBooks and nearly anything else to your target audience when you have their email address.

How can one make that list? Here's how

1. Choose a trusted and reliable email marketing service like MailChimp and Aweber. They provide a complete solution to all of your needs in email marketing which includes automating sign-ups as well as shooting emails, and providing figures. Based on your needs and preferences, you can select an annual subscription cost or a fee based on the quantity of emails that are sent.

2. Distribute highly useful or useful lead magnets as well as free data. This could be a piece of report, information or checklist that's not readily accessible on the internet. It should be the product of a thorough study or a source of information that isn't widely known of.

For example, if you run a blog on weddings, then you could publish an entire listing with the titles "top 50 budget friendly destination wedding hotspots for 2017" or "the ultimate wedding planning checklist" or "10 wedding speech ideas." People are awestruck by suggestions, ideas and lists that help make it easier to research.

In the same way, if your blog is about earning profits online, then you could write a report on the areas of interest or content that impresses the social media audience or headline/email templates they can utilize to reach out to their readers.

Offer up secrets that people aren't likely to share If you're looking to get your readers to exchange their email address in exchange. Attract interest of your target audience by providing them with an opportunity to earn their trust that's hard to reject.

3. You should ask for only the minimum of information when you fill out an opt-in

page. If it is taking longer people to input their details and provide their information, the greater the chances that they will end up absconding. Make sure you only ask for their email email and their name if you want to make your email more personal. Don't request any additional information if you're looking for higher rate of conversion. Opt-in form forms can be placed on your blog by copying an easy-to-use code supplied by the provider of email marketing services.

4. Utilize other lists to make your own. If you have a blog whose mailing list can benefit from the products or services that you promote, ask the blogger's owner to write content for their monthly newsletter.

You can also make an article in another publication in exchange for giving the blogger/owner a special service. Consider drafting or revising an announcement for a press release, or even creating an array of posts on social media. They'll be happy to include your name in their newsletters or write a piece on the subject if they receive something worthwhile for it.

A lot of affiliate and internet marketers are plagued by this "it's a dog eat dog world out here" syndrome. Find ways to cooperate instead of competing. Utilize the talents of others and their audience to form mutually beneficial partnerships. In this way, you will not just be able to survive but also conquer the market that is affiliate marketing. Always keep an eye out for opportunities to collaborate. Expand your reach by looking into other's users.

5. Create a special social media contest, promo or giveaway. In order to be eligible for the giveaway or contest users must provide their email addresses. If you've established a large presence on social media this is a great chance to convert your followers into mail-order subscribers.

Provide informative digital or physical items related to your blog's topic. The aim is to attract people who will be truly attracted by your affiliate promotion. Do not overdo this, however, or you'll receive a flood of useless sign-ups after you've earned the rewards.

6. The biggest errors affiliate marketers make when they create their lists is to try to sell their products with every mail. The main goal for this listing is convince the people you have who are on your list to purchase from you. Selling with every single mail seems like a completely selfish idea. It will lead to a significant drop in subscribers which will further reduce your profit.

Make sure you provide information for free every now and then to keep people who are on your mailing list. Offer them an incentive to keep coming back by providing value for free over the hard sell. This can include marketing emails that are pre-selling. Sometimes, you can sign up to them to freebies, such as an eBook or a few subscriptions/tools for free that will aid them. It's a great method to show appreciation for their participation in your list.

As a general rule, set aside two-thirds of your email for free information (newsletters or free reports, etc.).) and one-third for sales that are extremely aggressive.

7. Include an opt-in form on the blog's About Us page. About pages offer one of the highest rates of opt-in on blogs. If people click on the About page to find out how to use your site, they're typically interested in learning more about the blog and. If they're convinced that they'll benefit from your blog, they're prepared to sign up immediately. If you don't have an opt-in form in the first paragraphs of your About Us page, it's an opportunity that's missed.

8. Introduce new verticals. Don't limit yourself to one segment or vertical in the process of creating lists. For example, if, for instance, you're a blogger who runs an online blog that is focused on earning income online, you could make an effort to target photographers, writers and crafters as well as stay at home mothers and other groups that might be interested in earning money online with their talents. Make a list of different lists for each sector to allow you to target each section of your target market with relevant deals.

Repurpose your content to fit different market segments. You've already laid the foundations of your market. What you're now doing is adding more floor levels to your structure. It is possible to play in the details once you have the general skeleton.

Conclusion

Thanks for reading this article.

If you're lucky, you'll see that you don't require any additional details to make money from affiliate marketing.

Take what you've learned from this book and test how it affects you.

Don't give up too quickly!

Your first product review might not be a big success.

Even when you've been doing this for quite a while there will be "NADA" campaigns where you'll spend $30 and time, and not make any money for a couple of months.

This kind of thing happens. It's a commercial enterprise after all.

Do something today.

Be proactive and succeed!